House of the the Deaf Man

Andrea Porter and Tom de Freston

GATEHOUSE PRESS LTD

Published by
Gatehouse Press Limited
Bridge House, Bridge Street
Halesworth, Suffolk IP19 8AQ
www.gatehousepress.com

First Published in 2012 by
Gatehouse Press Limited

ISBN 978-0-9566385-3-3

Cover design by Lee Seaman

Printed in Great Britain by MPG Books, Bodmin and Kings Lynn

Acknowledgements

Andrea Porter

My thanks go to Tom and the team at Gatehouse Press who grasped our vision for this book and who keep the flame of the small independent publisher burning in dark financial times. A version of 'Consumed' was published in *Magma* in 2012. Thanks go to all those, especially Sian, who have supported me in my small obsession with Francisco Goya and his 'Black Paintings' and given me feedback on the poems. Finally I would like to give thanks for that old deaf man painting into the dark with candles round his hat.

Tom de Freston

Many thanks to Tom at Gatehouse for having the vision to make this project possible; Ian, Lee and Andy for bringing it to fruition in print; C4RD for giving me the Hatley residency; Henry and Josie at Breese Little; Pablo and Kiran for acting as sounding boards; my parents and the Millwood Hargraves for giving me studio space; and special thanks to Max Barton, as this project would not have been possible without his input. Most importantly, I would like to thank Andrea for approaching me to be involved and providing me with such an incredible body of poetry to respond to.

House of the Deaf Man
Quinta del Sordo

The Spanish artist Francisco Goya is regarded by some as the last of the 'Old Masters' of European art. His work provides a vital link between the Romantic period and modern art. His many prints that ridiculed the Church, the state and the mores of the day, give a unique perspective on Spanish society of the period.

Between 1810 and 1820 Goya was creating 'The Disasters of War', eighty-two copper plates depicting the worst and bloody excesses of the uprising by the Spanish people against the Napoleonic regime, the subsequent Peninsular War and the suffering of the ordinary people through famine, disease and loss of freedom. However these etchings and aquatints were regarded as so seditious and shocking that no one would risk publishing prints until long after his death. Partly due to these and some of his paintings such as 'The Second of May', Goya is also seen by many as the first true war artist, prepared to portray war, its realities and its consequences in graphic detail.

In 1814 Goya was brought before the Inquisition on charges of obscenity for his painting of The Naked Maja. The painting was confiscated and not shown in public again until years later. In that same year, a report was commissioned by the government and presented to the Inquisition and the King about Goya's apparent compliant behaviour during the French occupation of Spain.

In 1819 at the age of seventy-two Goya moved into a house situated in the countryside on the outskirts of Madrid near the Manzanares River. This house was already called Quinta del Sordo (House of the Deaf Man) after a previous occupant, but by this time Goya himself was also totally deaf. His deafness was caused by a serious illness he suffered twenty-six years earlier. Nothing is conclusively known about the nature of this illness but some believe that the high lead content of the paint he used may have contributed to his becoming ill.

During the five-year period that Goya lived in the house with his young housekeeper Leocadia Weiss and her daughter Rosario (believed by some to be Goya's child), he proceeded to paint a series of fourteen paintings directly onto the walls of his dining room and sitting room. These paintings have come to be known as 'The Black Paintings'. These works were never intended to be seen by the public, or for that matter to survive, as Goya well knew that oils applied directly onto thin plaster on adobe brick walls would result in the paintings decaying.

The paintings are as close as we can come to seeing into the private world of the artist; what obsessed him and what drove him in the last few years of his life. At this point in his life, Goya was thought to be in deep despair about the social and political situation in Spain and his own deafness and growing infirmity (his sight was also beginning to fail).

Whilst still remaining an official court painter and receiving a stipend from the royal coffers, he and Leocadia Weiss were also known to support the liberal movement in Spain. From 1820 to 1823 there was a liberal uprising against Ferdinand VII and the king was kept under virtual house arrest. In 1823 the French army entered Spain and reinstated Ferdinand as an absolute monarch. Ferdinand then proceeded to exact a cruel and bloody retribution against all those who has supported the liberal cause. This eventually led to Goya deciding to go into exile in France in 1825 during a brief period of amnesty.

When Goya left the house in 1825 for France, he gave the house to his grandson, no doubt expecting these paintings to fade and decay or be painted over. Goya died in France three years later. Goya never wrote about or acknowledged the existence of these 'Black Paintings' or gave them names, in this book they are referred to by the names attributed by art historians. It is only thanks to the art of the conservators that these paintings survive. They were lifted from the walls and transferred to canvas in 1874 and exhibited in the Prado Museum where they remain.

Artists' Statements

Andrea Porter

Over ten years ago I was in London and wandered by chance into the Haywood Gallery. There happened to be an exhibition of Goya's prints and drawings. As I walked around I was mesmerised. The Goya I had come across was the Goya of the Spanish court, with grand set pieces and formal portraits, but here was a very different artist. I began to seek out other work by Goya and read about the man and his times. The more I read and looked at his work the more I began to see a complex man, a man full of contradictions and strange hypocrisies but whose fears, nightmares and dreams were still very relevant to our current times. My reactions to Goya's highly personal 'Black Paintings' has been a long journey into his world and mine. The power of the visual speaks for itself; the word in response has to say something other, something that steps through that visual to another place.

I have sought to let these fourteen paintings be the beginning of a journey leading me to explore both Goya's world and my own, and question aspects of the times we live in. The continuing marvel of words is that they live in a space that is created by the listener and the writer together; marks on a page weave together sound, imagination and echoes of our own personal history. I have chosen a variety of forms; the sonnet, terza rima, rhyming couplets, free verse to reflect and explore the different worlds Goya's paintings suggest to me. The paintings have at times almost created the form the poem takes in that intimate dance between rhyme, rhythm, sound, tone and image that Ekphrasis can create.

The joy of the collaboration on this project for me has been seeing how, from images painted by an artist on the walls of his house nearly two hundred years ago, words and art can be energised to present a different dimension and experience that is as relevant to our present world as Goya's work continues to be.

Tom de Freston

This is not an illustration of Goya's time in the 'Quinta del Sordo' or a modernising of his 'Black Paintings'. Instead both of these sources have provided reference points for the building of a new world. The eroticism, mysticism and horror of the black paintings and Goya's deafness as a cruel physical manifestation of a wider set of psychological and biographical contradictions have taken central roles. Andrea's poetry gave me an opportunity to find new ways into Goya and his work, populating my mind with new characters and voices.

This ekphrastic engagement has allowed us to try and create a world which is elliptical, maddening and noisy, with time and space as an accordion, opening and collapsing to shifting rhythms, a fractured and fragmented realm with signs and signifiers destabilised. The current social and political climate is given nods with Saturn reincarnated as Bashar al-Assad and Rupert Murdoch, the puppet master, the model for a series of theatrical masks.

More broadly the violence and pornography are seen as interchangeable commodities from a 'society of the spectacle'. Goya's grotesques are replaced by a new cast of modernised monsters. A bastardised form of Christian Iconography appears in the form of a zombified Jesus turning the crucifixion into a dance at the disco of death, whilst the four horseman of the Apocalypse are a hybrid chorus line at the endscene of a bad Bollywood movie. A single falling figure nods at the Deposition whilst the same figure becomes Auden's beast which repeats itself in a swirling Last Judgment scene, the strict patternation of which seems more akin to William Morris wallpaper and the Rorschach test.

Art History becomes a compost heap of reference points. Goya's most violent scenes, Titian's *The Flaying of Marsyas*, Caravaggio's entombment and Gericault's *Raft of the Medusa* are all restaged in domestic settings. The screaming horse head from Picasso's *Guernica* nods to the terror of war, the collapsing of ideologies and the absurdity of an increasingly unstable psychological state. All the reference points above are lifted, mutated and restaged.

The safety of the domestic is polluted to create something unhomely, familiar but strange and akin to Freud's notion of the *Unheimlich*. The desire is to create a type of poetic and visual theatre where seemingly safe spaces are interrupted and infested by a white noise of psychological unrest and alienation similar to Brecht's notion of *Verfiemdungseffekt*.

Welcome to the *House of the Deaf Man*, we hope you will enjoy the show.

Prologue

Here in the house of the deaf man
the crow can sing, the walls can fly.

Here in the house of the deaf man
lips are the servant of the eye.

Here in the house of the deaf man
the word for other is silence.

Here in the house of the deaf man
air carries the weight of light.

Here in the house of the deaf man
a truth is as loud as the lie.

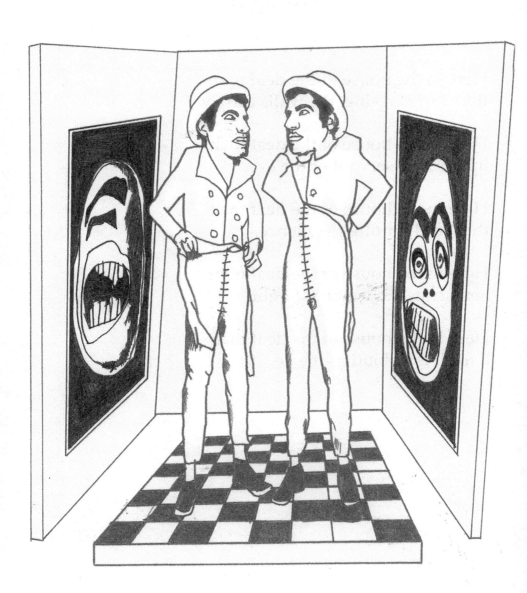

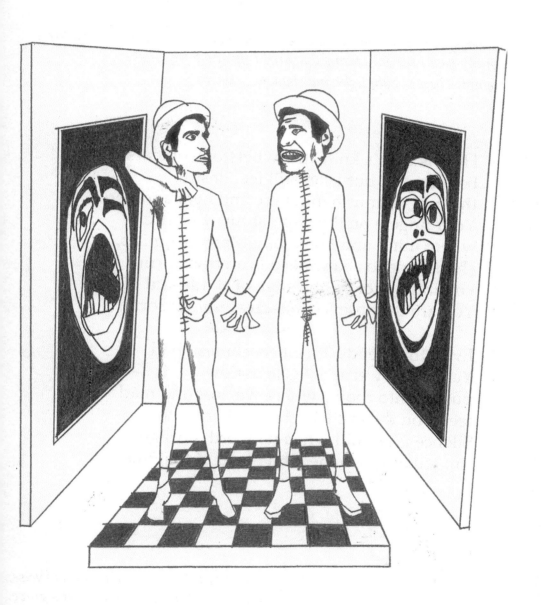

Negative Space

*'Always lines, never forms! But where do they find these lines in Nature!
For my part I see only forms that are lit up and forms that
are not. There is only light and shadow.' - Goya*

Here is time's knife, the whetstone of tears
between us, but I can still feel desire,
the heat of your hand, here and here and here.
Your fingers on the nape of my neck fire
where mind and body join. Marrow ignites,
chars bone to charcoal so I can transform
you into space on the edge of shade and light.
You are the absence that creates your form.

Everything ends, I have, becomes I had.
Yet memory erupts; its lava flow
pushes into rooms where we, lost and mad,
teeter on the brink of this dark inferno.
Silence is so cold when no word, no sign,
can tell or grasp the white-heat of that line.

*After the 'Black Painting' of Leocadia Weiss,
his mistress, leaning on the artist's grave.*

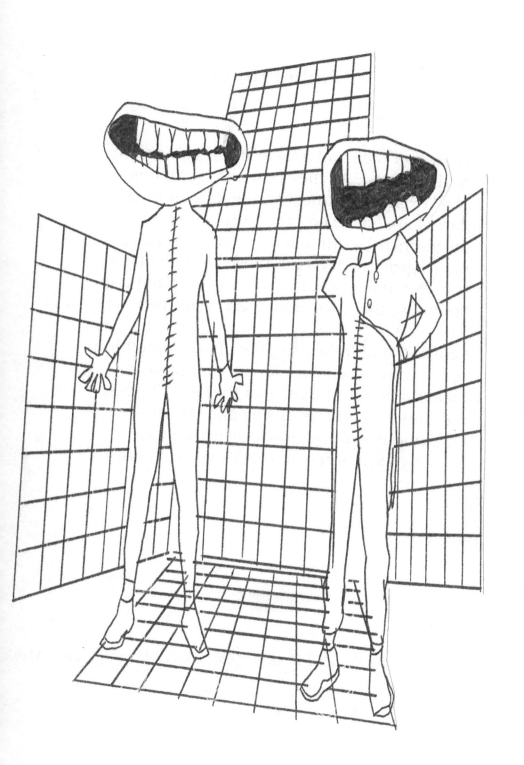

Sole Provider

To have a wife and a lover in the same room
is disquieting. As they talk and laugh together
I feel excluded, almost shunned, as if the joke
they share has to be some story about me;
the paunch I seem to have now, nose hair,
my in-growing toe-nail, those strange itches.
Is my sexual prowess after a night in the pub
bound by the rules of our secret confessions?

I confess that if they snigger about something
or someone else, I would feel excluded.
I should be the epicentre of their small lives,
the source of their meaning and pleasure.
My hand is slipping towards my crotch,
I am my own best solace in times of stress.

After the Black Painting 'Two Women Laughing and a Man'.

Consumed

In the dining room I have finished the grasping hands,
the air is thick with the smell and even my deaf ears
detect the high notes of putrefaction that coat the wall.

The eyes bother me, the necessity for a shade of white
too desperate for my palette makes the mixing of paint
another exercise in the toxic arts. The lead has stoppered
the jug of my brain enough to make the chemistry risky.

I have studied the priest in the inn eating a leg of lamb
to get the right degree of lean into the meat of the body.

The half erect penis may cause guests a little trouble.
All this power must be underlined by a sexual thrill,
besides this hard-on is only for private consumption.

Flesh that springs from our own loins is sweetest,
tender with all the hopes we baste them with.
What does he taste, this father; ripeness of muscle,
juices of a heart yet to feel the treacherous moment?
Is it salted with tears, the most ancient preservation?

Death is easily spat out but you need a strong stomach
when it comes to swallowing the whole corpus of love.

If I stop for lunch, the paint will congeal like blood.

After the Black Painting 'Saturn Devouring His Son'.

After

When you go to the supermarket
place my head in your wire basket
as you wander the aisles of meat.
Be careful my hair does not brush
the sign of two for the price of one.
Let check-out girls catch my eye.

Keep me close and always visible,
you never know when you will need
to raise me up as a bloody trophy,
to rouse shoppers from their torpor.
Never take lightly the authority given
when you show what victory means.

Guard me from thieves.
If I were stolen how could you prove
that a god and right and butchery are,
and always will be, on your side?
Insure me, but a policy of like for like
may cost far more than you can pay.

Post my decapitation up on YouTube,
followers want to see the neck bowed,
the thought severed from the deed.
Become the poster-girl for deliverance,
the strong woman's role in pay-back,
the lesson about listening to a deity.

Artists never see the flicker in the eyes
as you hack and saw through bone.
'Two blows' was their hyped publicity.
Most portray the moment before,
the moment after; the moment itself
disappears up the magician's sleeve.

Speak softly to me at three a.m.
Whisper sweet names you gave me.
Tell me other secrets; I know
about the knife you use to prise
my fingers from your heart,
the axe I take to your soul.

After the Black Painting 'Judith and Holifernes'.

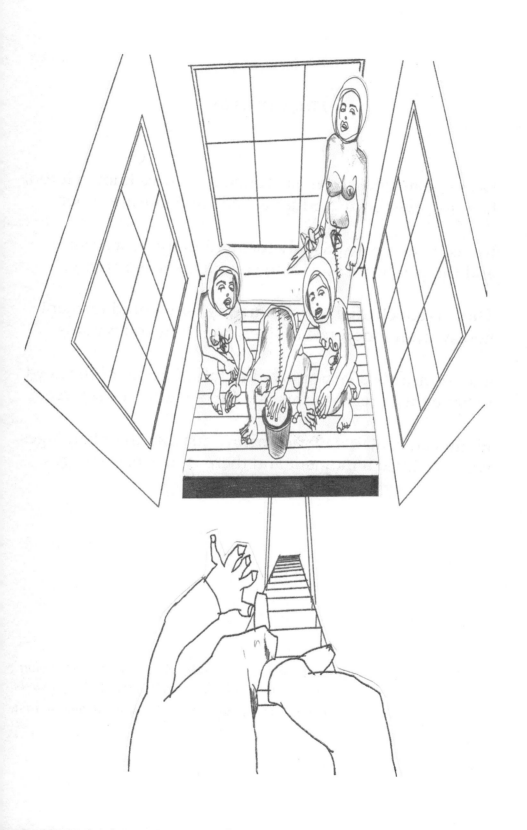

Inquisition

Desire, that silky red mist. Touch it. You've known it too,
hanging over crumpled hotel beds into late afternoon.

It's as if we are exquisitely tortured in this last scene
and the wet heat of our skin conducts the electricity.

There is shock after shock, the way you would torment
heresy from innocence until each arching jolt repents

and we are absolved of love but found guilty of the need
to have this, precisely this. Rise above guilt, be set free.

Flight can heal. Let worlds below gnaw at their bandages,
we have lived a moment and there is no sin, no wages.

After the Black Painting 'Asmodea' or 'The Fantastic Vision'.
Asmodea is the female version of Asmodeus,
one of the seven rulers of hell and the demon of lust.

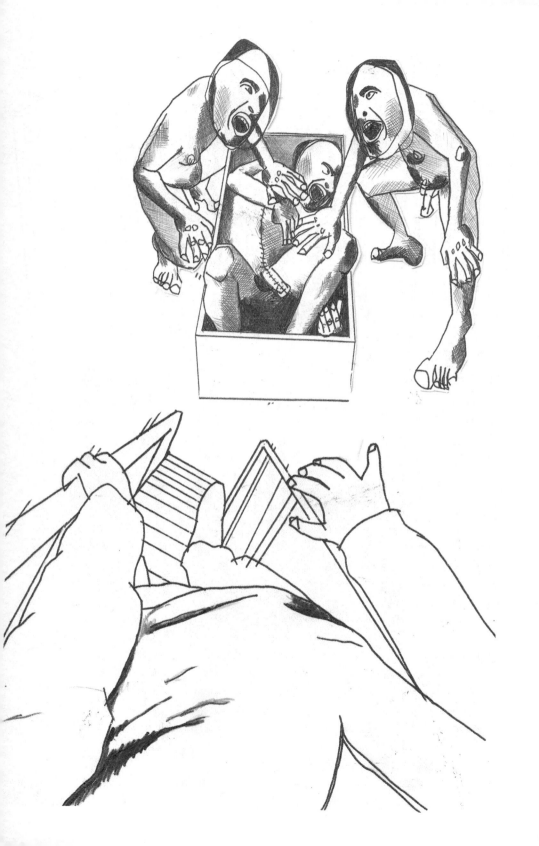

Pap

For Rupert Murdoch

We like soup, it slips down easy,
saves us gumming away at stuff
that will never break down
to something we can swallow.

We like spoons, no sharp edges,
nothing that can cut a finger
or prod us with sharp tines.
He can hang one from his nose.

We can amuse ourselves for hours
with just that one small trick.
We don't ask for much, just pap
and time for simple pleasures.

After the Black Painting 'Two Old Men Eating Soup'.

The Art of the Cudgel

It must be grown from that first apple tree,
a hand-me-down pip of all knowledge.
The grain of right and wrong will strengthen
the club, give it dead weight and an edge.

The best saplings should be planted in dust,
fed on bone meal and flakes of dried blood.
Force tender roots to fumble through strata,
through all the histories down to the flood.

When it stands upright, as high as two men,
pick a stout branch and ignore any knots;
complexities only add to its strength.
The best time is spring before the sap rots.

Whittle and fashion it under full moons,
for here the cycles and tides are born.
Seal in this rush to become and undo
with varnish distilled from briars and thorns.

Polish it well so it reflects who you are.
Practise until you and it are a whole.
Club and man must grow from one seed,
blind to the nature of which has control.

After The Black Painting 'Two Men Fighting with Cudgels'.

The Ultimate Men's Book Club

'When the fight was over, nothing was solved, but nothing mattered. We all felt saved.' - Fight Club

We band of brothers read
and bond over the page.
We abstain from Kindles
as this does not feed
our need for the eroticism
of a yielding spine,
those cool skins of paper,
the pheromone of ink.

Sometimes we stage fights
down in the library cellar.
There is much to be said
for bruises, broken bones.
the honed use of physicality
as the means of deciding
the quality of dystopian
Sci-Fi versus John Keats.
It is more meaningful
than those balloon debates.

There is always honour
in defending a book.
Ideas, imagined worlds,
truths and half truths already
have a bar code written
in someone's blood.

After The Black Painting 'Men Reading'.

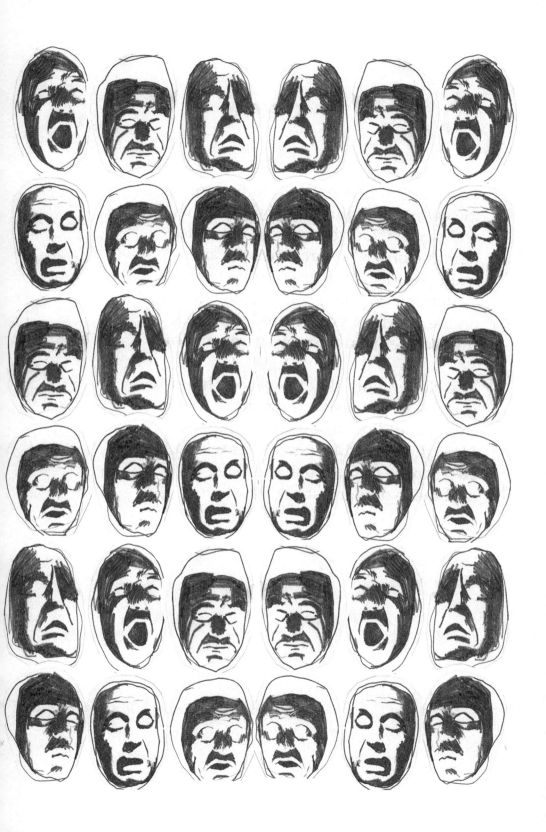

Cleave

Come close. Listen, listen to my voice,
the chant that murmurs low at night
and warms your body from the inside.
I am the one who wrenches the air
from your lungs in quickening jerks.
Watch my writhing image scroll down
on the inside of your closed lids. Lick
the picture from your lips and swallow.

The cloven hoof that takes your hand
is light, so practised in the art of touch
that it could be mistaken for fingers.
Here the dark slits in my eyes widen,
two candle flames rush to fill the void,
and those demons stir at your core.

After the Black Painting 'The Great He-Goat'.

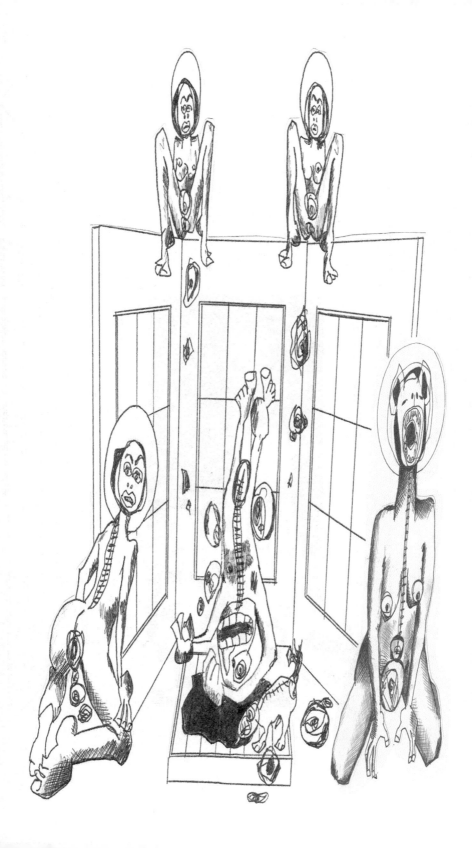

Mammon to the Mendicant Banker

*'Our banking system grew by accident; and whenever something happens
by accident, it becomes a religion.'* - Walter Wriston, US banker.
'No comment.' - Spokesman for Royal Bank of Scotland prior to
government bail-out.

You may think a vow of silence lends
you an air of piety and quiet dignity,
nothing to report, all receive and no send.

But I, at least, can react to the anxieties
of the common man who tries to get by
with just a habit in a consumer society.

In an age when demand outstrips supply,
I know that your blind and stubborn trust
in manna is madness, it's foolish to rely

on any gods for soft soap, a bonus, a crust
of bread. Keeping this faith will not work;
self-delusion is the mirror of self-disgust.

I and others may see your smile as a smirk,
that you have a secret you will not share.
I beg for us both now as if it were a perk

of the job, a reward apart from prayer,
but yours are fast become a stale routine,
like my blessing to the taker. I swear,

if the giving of my meagre word means
anything, you would still trade me
for a handful of futures, magic beans.

After the Black Painting 'Two Old Monks'.

Pilgrims

We have worn out our soles
traipsing after an empty hand
and return to ask for something
we are not prepared to carry.
What we hold now darkens us
to a rain soaked smudge,
one animal, whose black spine
shudders down a village street.

Something ripped away like Velcro
is all sudden sound and parting.
We bend under the press of rain,
clutch at slicks of street light
but the grace, the weight of each day,
is all we may bear on this road.

After the Black Painting 'Procession of the Holy Office'.

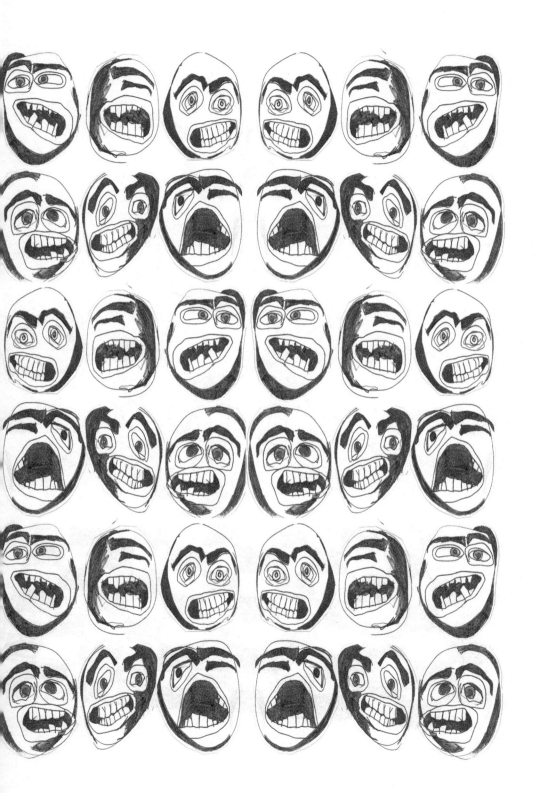

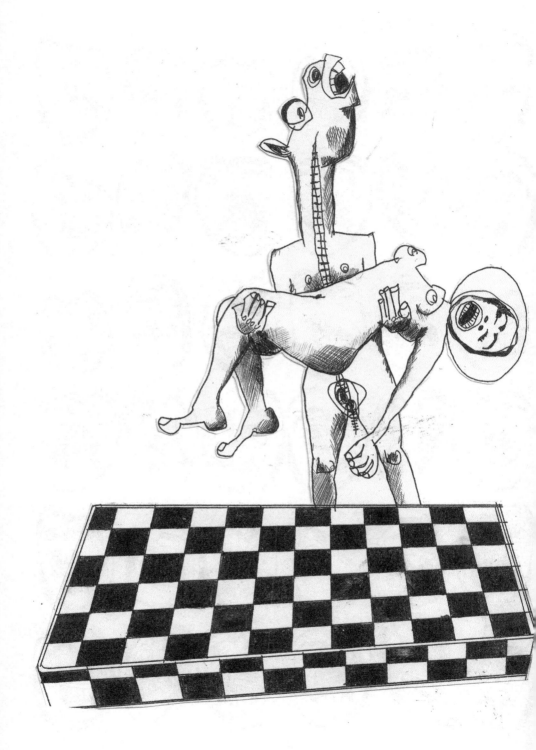

With the lights out it's less dangerous

That last time in the pub there was a band playing
in the back room, a bad cover of Nirvana.
Kurt Cobain was being strangled and died again.

You poked at spilt wine, trickling like opened veins
across the table top, damming it near the ashtray,
drawing it out to the edge. Out in the night it rained.

A couple rushed through the door, slick with it all.
The band thrashed louder as the boy wiped drops
of water from her young face. Silence could fall

and they would be unaware, the room hushed
for them already. Doodling boxes on the beer mat,
I talked. Something came out but I crushed

the words up with the crisp packet, the dead ends
of cigarettes and they didn't sound like mine.
Now in my head I followed the band, blending

all of us, all of it, into one sound and your finger
pushed it over the edge and it started to drip
onto the floor. If we had been these strangers

I would have avoided your eye, yet we were.
Similar faces but older, too many worlds,
too hard a game of small goodbyes conferred

on your eyes a weariness and on mine mistrust.
You stood up to leave; in the light or in the dark
being with you was always far more dangerous.

After the Black Painting 'Pilgrimage to San Isidro'.

40

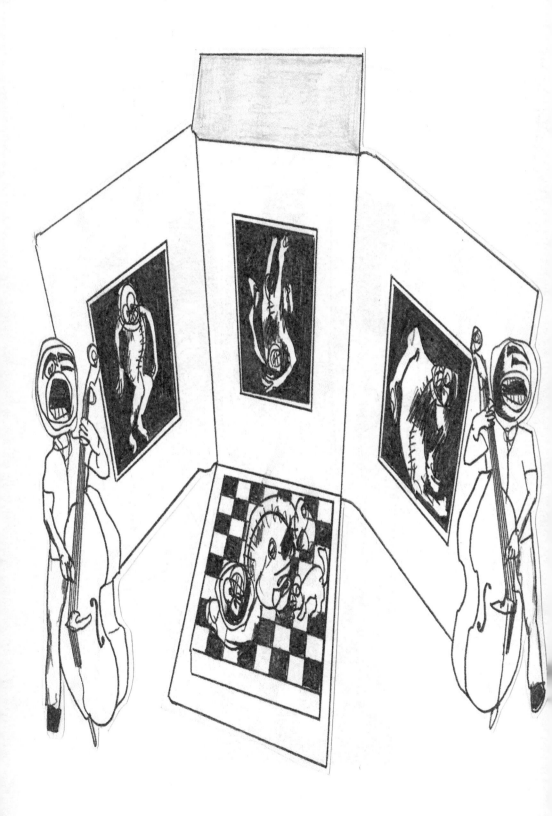

Lesson

The swimming lesson has begun.
No, you won't need arm-bands
or in your case leg-bands.
Head up, that's how it's done.

That ominous cracking sound?
Well your vertebrae can cope.
Keep your eyes fixed on a point
way up there, on higher ground.

No point in setting the bar too low.
A challenge? Yes, but attainable.
You have never ridden a bicycle
but think pedalling and just let go.

Why murky water? So you don't see
the darker crap below. It could
make the art of keeping afloat
far more tricky than it has to be.

After the Black Painting 'The Dog'.

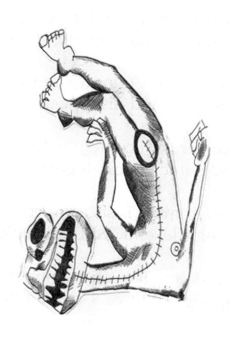

On Close Examination

She spins, I measure and that one cuts;
even meddling gods are afraid of us.

Here we loom over you, older than time,
here before you inched from the slime

and knew the endless minutes and years
that plummet past and disappear.

You, old man, are not content with three.
Our face and name have a degree

of licence but number is sacrosanct.
Beginning, middle, end. You can bank

on birth, life, death, it's solid symmetry.
Two's company but three's a guarantee

that time on this earth remains unravelled.
It can be short, shit and badly handled

but the thread is spun until it's snipped.
You know about death, written its script

into your brush, drawn the cut strands
hung from trees in this bleeding land.

But this fourth fate with the spy-glass
hints quality control will have to pass

our handiwork. Will your short span,
show fuck-ups made by another man?

I see her glass is turned towards the door,
beyond which are all the other flaws

but here is the reminder to own your fate,
an art more difficult than mastery of paint.

After the Black Painting 'The Fates'.

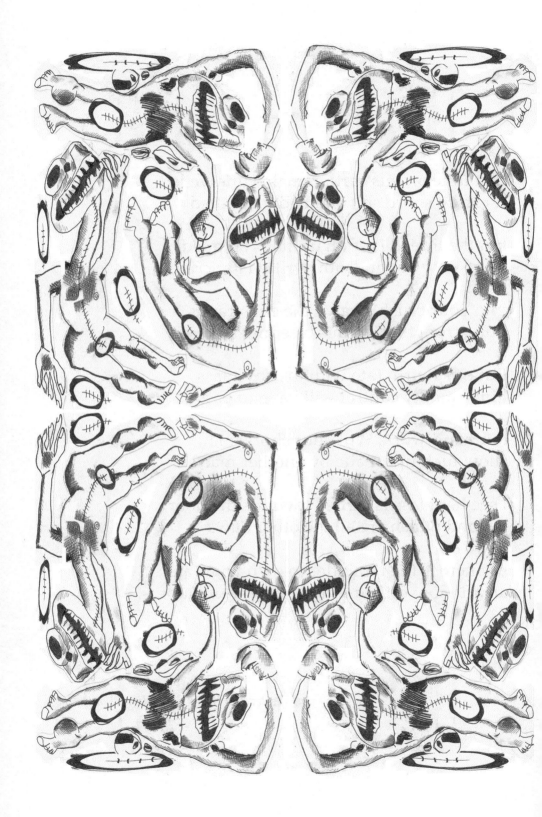

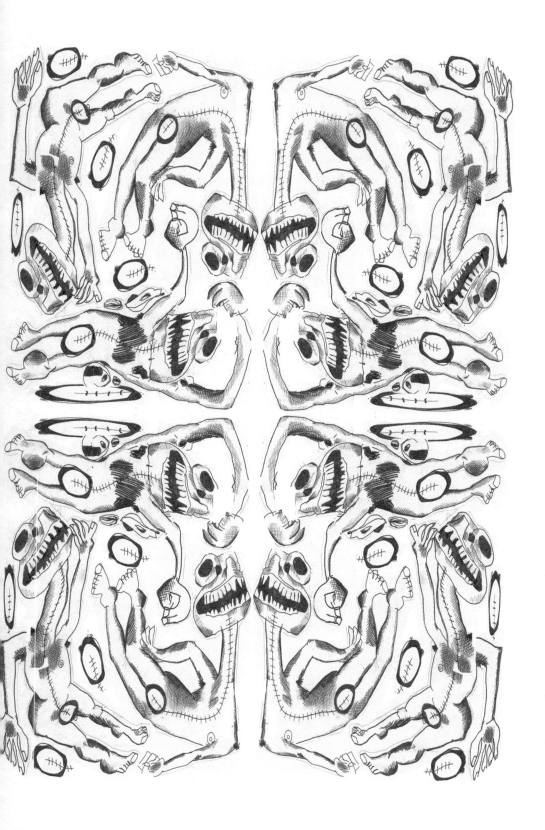

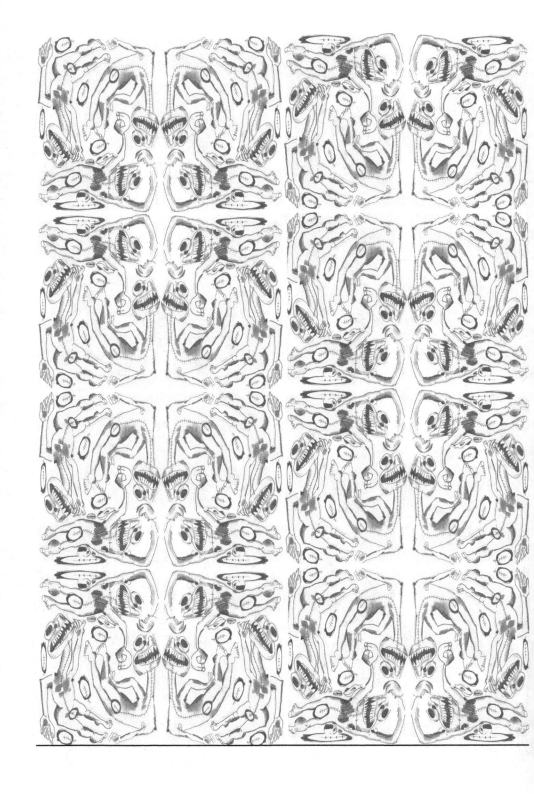

Epilogue in the Town Cafe

'Fantasy abandoned by reason produces impossible monsters: united with her, she is the mother of the arts and the origin of their marvels.' - Goya

I spot him in the window seat
looking back into the shadows.
I can see that his hand twitches,
as if the need to move and capture
troubles his fingers like chilblains.
His mug of coffee is barely touched.

He stares at a man without teeth
slumped over a pasty who grins
at a baby in a buggy. This man pulls
in his lips, gurns to amuse the child,
who howls and opens up its own
toothless hole to suck in a terror.

I can see the old man's hand burn
as if to blacken and scorch the stick
he stirs with. Each muscle and nerve
recall the days of the massacre,
the dead he painted with a spoon.
He memorises the child's mouth.

He studies his watch, The White Hart
is not open yet. He undresses
the woman who wipes the table.
The Big Issue man grows a skull,
a couple morph into donkeys.
I tap on the window, ghost tremors

in the pane draw his eyes to the glass.
He looks through the light and me
to a point where all things join,
vanish into one small brush stroke.
It's a market day and old women
with bloated ankles pour from a bus.

He hobbles to the door and opens it,
steps into worlds of fruit and veg,
of cheap pants and mobile phones.
The noise is mass and movement,
silence played on pipes of charcoal.
The deaf man hears the roar if it all.

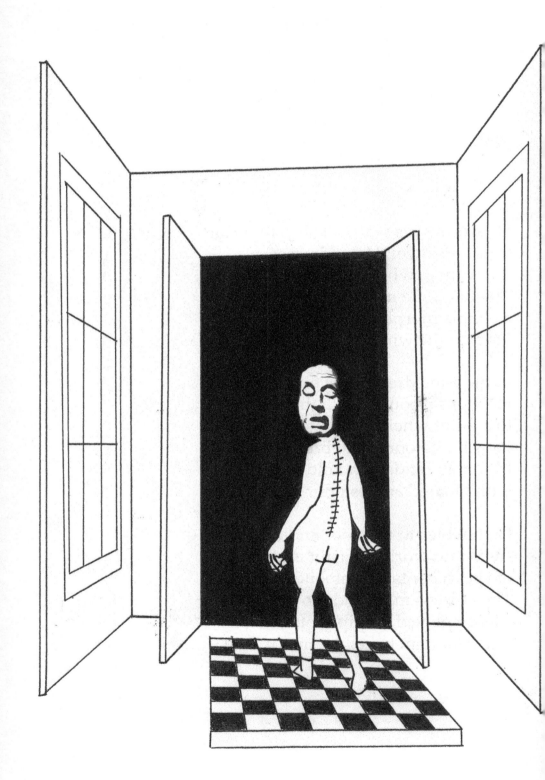